CONGREGATION FOR INSTITUTES
OF CONSECRATED LIFE AND SOCIETIES
OF APOSTOLIC LIFE

NEW WINE IN NEW WINESKINS

THE CONSECRATED LIFE AND ITS ONGOING CHALLENGES SINCE VATICAN II

GUIDELINES

All documents are published thanks to the generous support of the members of the Catholic Truth Society

CATHOLIC TRUTH SOCIETY
PUBLISHERS TO THE HOLY SEE

CONTENTS

Nobody puts new wine into old wineskins; if he does,
the wine will burst the skins, and the wine is lost and the skins too.
No! New wine, fresh skins!

(*Mk 2:22*)

First published 2017 by The Incorporated Catholic Truth Society 40-46 Harleyford Road London SE11 5AY. Libreria Editrice Vaticana omnia sibi vindicate iura. Sine eiusdem licentia scripto data nemini liceat hunc textum denuo imprimere aut in aliam linguam vertere. Copyright © 2017 Libreria Editrice Vaticana, Città del Vaticano. This edition © 2017 The Incorporated Catholic Truth Society.

ISBN 978 1 78469 202 5

INTRODUCTION

The Congregation for Institutes of Consecrated Life and Societies of Apostolic Life held the Plenary session of the Dicastery from 27th-30th November 2014 on the theme *"New wine in new wineskins. Consecrated life 50 years after Lumen Gentium and Perfectae Caritatis"*. It focused on the journey that the consecrated life has made in the post-conciliar period, while trying to summarise its ongoing challenges.

These *Guidelines* are a product of what emerged in the plenary session and in subsequent reflection, and were created following the many encounters held during the *Year of Consecrated Life* that brought consecrated men and women from all over the world together in Rome, at the See of Peter.

The Church's Magisterium has accompanied the lives of consecrated people continuously since the Second Vatican Council. This Dicastery, in particular, has provided great points of reference and value: the Instruction *Potissimum Institutioni* (1990), *Fraternal Life in Community* (1994), *Starting Afresh from Christ* (2002), *The Service of Authority and Obedience Faciem Tuam* (2008), and *Identity and Mission of the Religious Brother in the Church* (2015).

These *Guidelines* are brought together as "an exercise in *evangelical discernment*, wherein we strive to recognise – in the light of the Spirit – a call which God causes to resound in the historical situation itself. In this situation, and also though it, God calls"[1] the consecrated men and women of our time, because "all of us are asked to obey his call to go forth from our own comfort zone in order to reach all the 'peripheries' in need of the light of the Gospel"[2].

It is an exercise in ecclesial discernment through which consecrated men and women are called to undergo new changes so that ideals and doctrine become real in our lives: systems, structures, *diaconia*, styles, relationships and language. Pope Francis highlights the need for this verification: "Realities are more important than ideas. [...] Realities simply are, whereas ideas are worked out. There has to be a continuous dialogue between the two, lest ideas become detached from realities. It is dangerous to dwell in the realm of words alone, of images and rhetoric"[3].

---

[1] Francis, Apostolic Exhortation *Evangelii Gaudium* (November 24, 2013), 154.

[2] *Ibid*, 20.

[3] *Ibid*, 231.

Even in the wide-ranging and rich process of *accomodata renovatio* taking place in the post-Council period, consecrated life can still find itself presented with ongoing challenges that must be faced "with determination and an eye to the future"[4].

In the perspective of an exercise of discernment, these *Guidelines* intend to find unsuitable practices, point out blocked processes, pose concrete questions, and ask questions about the structures of relationships, government and formation in regard to the real support given to the evangelical form of life of consecrated persons.

They are *guidelines* to test, with *parresìa*, the *wineskins* made to preserve the *new wines* that the Spirit continues to give to his Church, inciting us to initiate changes through concrete action in the short and long term.

---

[4] *Ibid*, 58.

FOR NEW WINE, NEW WINESKINS

THE *LOGION* OF JESUS

1. A word from the Lord Jesus can illuminate the journey of consecrated life in the face of the challenges of our time and in the spirit of the renewal called for by the Second Vatican Council: *new wine* in *fresh skins* (*Mk* 2:22). This sapiential expression from the Lord is attested for in all of the Synoptics, which place it in the context of the initial phase of Jesus's public activity. Mark the Evangelist places it right at the heart of the first criticisms from the Pharisees of Capernaum in regard to Jesus's freedom and autonomy to act (Mk 2:18-22). Matthew presents the scene of this *logion* earlier, as if to seal the prophetic charge of the centrality of mercy in his words and gestures (*Mt* 9:16-17). Luke is even more precise in contextualising this provocation, underlining the impossibility of conversing with the old mentalities (*Lk* 5:36-39). This evangelist notes that the piece of cloth is torn *from the new cloak* (for Matthew, it is *unshrunken* cloth) to be sewn onto the *old cloak*. This clumsy operation provokes a double ruin (*Lk* 5:36), and Luke adds yet another telling phrase: *Nobody who has been drinking old wine wants new. "The old is good" he says* (*Lk* 5:39).

All three Synoptic Evangelists find it important to underline the newness of the style in which the Lord Jesus, while revealing the merciful face of the Father to the world, places himself at a critical distance from the simple observance of customary religious schemes. Forgiving sins and embracing every person in the mystery of suffering, and even, of errancy, is a radical change. This change destabilises those who are used to the simple repetition of a scheme in which everything is already expected and understood. Not only does this attitude create embarrassment, but it becomes a reason for refusal from the very beginning. The style in which Jesus proclaims the Kingdom of God is based on the *law of freedom* (cf. *Jm* 2:12) which permits a new way of relating to people and concrete situations. This style has all the colour and flavour of a *new wine* that, however, risks tearing the *old wineskins*. This image clearly shows how institutional, religious, and symbolic forms must always be gaining *flexibility*. Without the necessary flexibility no institutional form, no matter how venerable, can withstand the tensions of life or respond to the appeals of history.

2. The simile used by the Lord Jesus is as simple as it is demanding. The wineskin in the short parable is a container made of soft leather that is still able to dilate, allowing the young wine to breathe as it continues to ferment. If, however, the wineskin were dry and stiff from the wear of time, then it would no longer be flexible enough to withstand the intense pressure of the new wine. It would break, causing the loss of both the wine and the wineskin. The Evangelist John will use the same metaphor of the *best wine* (*Jn* 2:10) served at the wedding at Cana to indicate the prophetic novelty of the joyous and lively proclamation of the Gospel. The *best wine* and the *new wine* thus become symbols of the actions and teachings of Jesus which cannot be kept in the old wineskins of secularised religious schemes that are incapable of opening themselves up to new promises. When the Evangelist Luke speaks about *good* (*chrestòs*) old wine, he is certainly referring to the attachment of the Pharisees and the leaders of the people to the standardised and rigid forms of the past. But maybe that's not all. Even second-generation Christians themselves have to deal with the tendency not to open up completely to the newness of the Gospel. The risk of giving in to the temptation of going back to the old ways of a world closed off by its own certainties and habits is always lurking. The temptation strategically to adapt oneself in order to avoid the continuous challenges involved in converting the heart has been present throughout the history of the Church.

The word of the Lord Jesus helps us take on the challenge of a change that requires acceptance, as well as discernment. We must create structures that are truly fit to preserve the innovative richness of the Gospel so that it can be experienced and put to the service of all, while preserving its quality and goodness. *New wine* must be left to ferment, almost breathe, inside the wineskin so that it can age properly and eventually be savoured and shared. The same is true of the symbol of the cloak and patch: a piece of cloth cannot be torn from a new cloak to patch up a worn-out cloak. By doing so, tension is put on the old cloak, causing it to fray even further and rendering the patch useless.

3. The Gospel message cannot be reduced to something purely sociological. Rather, it is a spiritual guideline that is always new. It requires the open-mindedness to imagine prophetic and charismatic ways to live the *sequela* of Christ through suitable, and possibly unprecedented, frameworks. There is a whole range of innovative *diaconia* experienced outside of the usual schemes that must also find a place in new institutional structures. These structures must be able to measure up to expectations and challenges. A renewal process that cannot affect and change the structures, in addition to hearts, will not produce real and lasting change. One must always bear in mind that a simple stretch, no matter how generous, can lead to rejection. Rejection means losing the excitement of the inevitable change that not only needs to be acknowledged, but experienced to the full, and certainly not merely endured or put up with.

If we apply this evangelical principle to what the Church went through in the moment of grace of the Second Vatican Council, we can truly speak of *new wine*. Under the guidance of the Holy Spirit, the Church, as the Lord's vineyard, was able to experience a renewed spiritual harvest through the contribution and generosity of all. We were all able to rejoice in the lively experiences of renewal that manifested in new catechetical itineraries, renewed models of holiness and fraternal life, renewed government structures, new theological currents, unimagined forms of solidarity and *diaconia*, etc: a true harvest that we can perceive with feelings of abundant and joyful gratitude. Nevertheless, all of these signs of renewal and forms of change co-exist – and this is also normal – with old habits that have been sanctified and fossilised. With their rigidity and inability, these habits resist actually adapting to this ongoing renewal. Conflicts, even severe conflicts, can arise from this co-existence of styles. From these conflicts emerge reciprocal accusations of not being *superlative wine* (*Sg* 7:10) but of being spoiled by *foaming wine* (*Ps* 75:9). There are even those who judge others as *sour grapes* (cf. *Is* 5:2) for not being faithful enough to what has always been established and tried. One should be neither upset nor discouraged by this. We cannot develop structures that are fit for true renewal without taking into account time to process and inevitable disputes along the way. Authentic and long-lasting changes are never automatic.

Normally, these changes have to face a whole range of resistance and setbacks. It must be recognised that this resistance is not always malicious or in bad faith. Today, more than fifty years after the conclusion of the Second Vatican Council, we must acknowledge that letting ourselves become upset and destabilised by the animating incitements of the Spirit is never painless. This certainly applies to the consecrated life and its seasons that, at times, may have more or fewer responses to the signs of the times and the inspirations of the Holy Spirit.

POST-CONCILIAR *RENEWAL*

4. A bit of history can illuminate and confirm our path as we look ahead and continue walking in the spirit of renewal established by the Council. Being aware of what we have experienced in this half-century becomes even more important if we want to understand the impetus in the words and gestures of Pope Francis.

The *accomodata renovatio* of life and the discipline of the institutes of consecrated life "for their needs in our time"[5] was an explicit request of the Second Vatican Ecumenical Council. The Council Fathers laid the theological and ecclesiological foundation for this *renewal* specifically in Chapter VI of the dogmatic Constitution *Lumen Gentium*[6]. In the Decree *Perfectae Caritatis*, they gave more appropriate directives and practical guidelines for the spiritual, ecclesial, charismatic and institutional *adaptation* of consecrated life in the Church. Out of the other conciliar texts, only the Constitution *Sacrosanctum Concilium* and the Decree *Ad Gentes* specified a few practical implications of some significance for religious life.

Half a century later, we can recognise, with satisfaction, that the effect of the conciliar *mens* on consecrated life has been particularly great. Their *style* of unanimous discernment and explorative attention generated highly effective impulses and methods for the *adaptation*. The first step towards this profound change was for consecrated life to understand anew

---

[5] Vatican Ecumenical Council II, Decree on the Adaptation and Renewal of Religious Life *Perfectae Caritatis*, 1

[6] Cf. Vatican Ecumenical Council II, Dogmatic Constitution on the Church *Lumen Gentium*, 43-47.

who it was. In the pre-conciliar period, religious life, in all of its forms and structures, represented the united and operational force for the life and mission of a militant Church seen to be in constant opposition to the world. In the new season of openness and dialogue with the world, consecrated life felt pushed to the forefront of exploring the co-ordinates of a new Church-world relationship to the benefit of the entire ecclesial body. This is one of the most inspirational and transformative themes of the Second Vatican Council announced by Saint John XXIII. Along these lines of dialogue and acceptance, consecrated life has normally, even if not always, willingly embraced the risks of this new adventure of openness, listening, and service. In order to really concretise their relational style and presence in the modern world marked by trust, consecrated life put its many charisms and its spiritual heritage into play, exposing itself and openly embracing new paths.

5. We can acknowledge that, in these fifty years that separate us from the conciliar event, all institutes of consecrated life have done their best to respond to the demands of Vatican II. The renewal effort was especially generous and creative in the first thirty years after the Council and even into the next ten years, although the rhythm had slowed down and the dynamism had become a little tired. Normative texts and institutional forms were revised; first, in response to the urging of the Council, and later, to conform to the regulations of the new *Code of Canon Law* (1983). Great effort was put forth by each religious family in rereading and interpreting the "original spirit of the institutes"[7]. This work had two main purposes: to faithfully guard "the mind and designs of the founders"[8] and "to propose anew the enterprising initiative, creativity and holiness of their founders and foundresses in response to the signs of the times emerging in today's world"[9].

The outcomes of all this effort to revise the identity, lifestyle and relative ecclesial mission were also accompanied by courageous and patient research into new formative itineraries that would be suitable

---

[7] Vatican Ecumenical Council II, Decree on the Adaptation and Renewal of Religious Life *Perfectae Caritatis*, 2.

[8] *CIC*, c. 578.

[9] John Paul II, Post-Synodal Apostolic Exhortation *Vita Consecrata* (25th March 1996), 37.

for the nature and charism of each religious family. Many aspects of the governing structures and the management of economic goods and activities were also adapted to "the modern physical and psychological circumstances of the members... to the necessities of the apostolate, the demands of the culture, and social and economic circumstances"[10].

6. After this brief glance at the history of the last fifty years, we can acknowledge, with humility, that consecrated life has exercised dwelling in the horizons of the Council with passion and exploratory audacity. We must thank God and each other, sincerely and truly, for the progress we have made on this journey.

The supreme Magisterium of the Popes has been of great support along this generous and laborious journey. Through various kinds of texts and interventions, the Pontiffs have regularly helped consolidate new convictions, discern new paths, and guide new choices regarding presence and service with wisdom and ecclesial sense in constant listening to the promptings of the Spirit. The Post-Synodal Apostolic Exhortation *Vita Consecrata* (1996), in which the best results of post-conciliar *adjustment* are accepted and confirmed, must be considered a document of exceptional theological, ecclesial and guiding value.

Contemplation and the fontal reference to the mystery of the Holy Trinity are of particular importance in *Vita Consecrata*: "The consecrated life proclaims what the Father, through the Son and in the Spirit, brings about by his love, his goodness and his beauty. In fact, 'the religious state reveals the transcendence of the Kingdom of God and its requirements over all earthly things. To all people it shows wonderfully at work within the Church the surpassing greatness of the force of Christ the King and the boundless power of the Holy Spirit'. [...] The consecrated life thus becomes one of the tangible seals which the Trinity impresses upon history, so that people can sense with longing the attraction of divine beauty"[11]. The consecrated life becomes *confessio trinitatis* even in its grappling with the challenge of fraternal life "whereby consecrated persons strive

---

[10] Vatican Ecumenical Council II, Decree on the Adaptation and Renewal of Religious Life *Perfectae Caritatis*, 3

[11] John Paul II, Post-Synodal Apostolic Exhortation *Vita Consecrata* (25th March 1996), 20.

to live in Christ with *one heart and soul (Ac* 4:32)"[12]. In this trinitarian perspective, we see the great challenge of unity emerge and the need for prayerful, testimonial and martyrial ecumenism as the best way forward for consecrated men and women: "Christ's prayer to the Father before his Passion, that his disciples may be one (cf. *Jn* 17:21-23), lives on in the Church's prayer and activity. How can those called to the consecrated life not feel themselves involved?"[13]

Even the hard-working and wise guidance of this Congregation offered, in many ways – *Instructions, Letters, Directives* – and with periodical vigilance, some guiding principles on how to persevere with authenticity through the conciliar *adaptation* and how to remain faithful, with unanimous discernment and prophetic audacity, to the ecclesial identity and function of the consecrated life.

This, however, does not mean denying fragility and fatigue, which are to be recognised and named so that the journey we have undertaken not only continues, but becomes even more radicalised in terms of fidelity and creativity. We must also take a realistic look at the new situations in which consecrated life is called to challenge and incarnate itself.

NEW PATHS CHALLENGE US

7. The rich multiplicity of *diaconia* exercised by consecrated life in recent decades has been radically reduced due to social, economic, political and scientific evolution. The same goes for state intervention in many sectors of work that were historically typical of religious people. All this has changed the way religious people relate to the context in which they live and their usual way of interacting with others. In the meantime, new and unprecedented emergencies have given rise to new needs that have yet to be responded to and that are knocking on the door of the creative faithfulness of consecrated life in all its forms.

New poverties challenge the conscience of many consecrated people and urge historic charisms to take on new forms of generous response in the face of new situations and the new rejects of history. From here, the rise of new forms of presence and service in the many existential

---

[12] *Ibid*, 21.

[13] *Ibid*, 100.

peripheries. We must not forget about the proliferation of volunteer initiatives in which men and women, lay and religious, are involved in a synergy that is rich in "renewed apostolic dynamism"[14], so as to "[render] more effective the response to the great challenges of our time, thanks to the combined contributions of the various gifts"[15]. This symphony is based on the rediscovery of the common baptismal root shared by all of Christ's disciples who are called to unite their efforts and imaginations to make this world more beautiful and liveable for all.

Many congregations, especially female congregations, have started focusing on the foundations in young Churches, and they have passed from almost entirely *monocultural* contexts to the challenge of *multiculturalism*. International communities were established that, for some institutes, represented the first courageous experience in leaving their geographic and cultural boundaries. Experiences of *diaconia* and presence were started in unknown or multi-religious contexts; new communities inserted themselves into difficult environments, often at the risk of various forms of violence. These experiences have brought about great changes within religious families, both as a cultural *ethos* to share and as Church models and innovative styles of spirituality. This exodus has naturally created problems for the traditional formative framework which was unsuitable for the new vocations and contexts. All of this is certainly a great asset, but it is also a source of much tension that, at times, has reached breaking point, especially in congregations with less missionary experience.

8. The modern evolution of society and cultures, which are undergoing rapid and extensive unexpected and chaotic changes, has also exposed consecrated life to the continual challenges of adjusting. This constantly requires new responses and it approaches crises of projectuality and charismatic profile. The sign of this crisis is the obvious effort being made. We must acknowledge that in some cases, it is a matter of being unable to pass from an ordinary administration (*management*) to a guide who measures up to the new situation in which it is important to act wisely. It is not an easy task to go from the simple administration of a

---

[14] *Ibid*, 55.

[15] *Ibid*, 54.

well-known situation to leading others towards unknown destinations and ideals with a conviction that generates real trust. It is not enough to focus on strategies of mere survival, but requires the necessary freedom to launch processes, as Pope Francis continues to remind us. A ministry to lead that can solicit real synodality by fostering a dynamism of synergy is becoming ever more necessary. Only in this communion of intents will it be possible to manage the transition with patience, wisdom and foresight.

Some matters have become more and more complex and paralyzing for consecrated life and its institutions over time. The situation of accelerated change risks entangling the consecrated life, forcing it to get by on emergencies instead of horizons. At times, it seems as though consecrated life is almost completely wrapped up in managing the day-to-day or in merely surviving. This way of facing reality is detrimental to a life that is full of meaning and capable of prophetic witness.

The constant management of increasingly compelling emergencies consumes more energy than one might think. Unfortunately, the risk is that one may get completely wrapped up in containing problems rather than imagining paths. The charismatic impulse of the Council seems almost to have failed in this frantic struggle. The great commitment to renewal and creativity seems to have been recently followed by stagnation with no way out just as we are being called upon openly to embrace new exoduses. In many cases, a fear of the future debilitates and devitalises that prophetic ministry – which Pope Francis insists upon[16] – that consecrated life is called to exercise in the Church for the good of all humanity.

9. At this point of the journey, it is healthy and necessary to stop and discern the quality and degree of maturation of the *new wine* that has been produced in the long season of post-conciliar renewal. Some questions arise. The first question concerns the harmony and coherence between the structures, organisms, roles and styles that have been around for some time and those that have been introduced in recent years to respond to the conciliar dictate[17]. The second question attempts to evaluate whether

---

[16] Francis, *Apostolic Letter* to all consecrated people on the occasion of the Year of Consecrated Life (21st November 2014).

[17] Cf. Vatican Ecumenical Council II, Decree on the Adaptation and Renewal of Religious Life *Perfectae Caritatis*, 2-4.

the elements of mediation in operation today in consecrated life are fit to embrace the most obvious changes and to support – in the metaphor of the *new wine* that ferments – its necessary transition towards full stability. Lastly, we can ask ourselves if what we savour and offer to drink is actually *new wine* that is full-bodied and wholesome? Or, despite all the good intentions and praiseworthy effort, is it wine that has been watered down to make up for the acids – the consequence of a bad harvest and poorly pruned vines?

These questions can be asked with simplicity and *parresìa*, without giving in to feelings of guilt which might block us further. We can take some time to look at what is going on inside the *wineskins* of our consecrated life. It is a matter of determining the quality of the *new wine* and the *best wine*, and not about placing blame or accusing. We are called to pour this wine, of which we are the loving keepers, for the joy of all, especially the poor and the little ones.

We must not be afraid to honestly acknowledge how, despite a series of changes, the old institutional framework struggles to give way to new models in a decisive manner. Perhaps the entire constellation of languages and models, values and duties, spirituality and ecclesial identity that we are used to has not yet left room to for the testing and stabilising of the new paradigm born of inspiration and post-conciliar practice. We are undergoing a period of necessary and patient revision of everything that makes up the heritage and identity of consecrated life inside the Church and before history. We must also indicate and interpret that tenacious resistance that had been hidden for a long time, but that has now reappeared explicitly in many contexts even as a possible response to an ill-concealed sense of frustration. In some of the realities of consecrated life, sometimes even relevant from a numerical point of view or from the point of view of available means, we are unable to accept the signs of the new. As we are used to the taste of *old* wine and reassured by proven modalities, we are not really open to any change unless it is substantially irrelevant.

10. After having presented and shared the state in which consecrated life currently finds itself, we would like to present some inconsistencies and resistances. This kind of sharing is being offered in truth and loyalty. We can no longer postpone the task of understanding together where the knot is

that needs to be untangled in order to come out of paralysis and overcome fears regarding the future. In addition to trying to name what is blocking that dynamism of growth and renewal that belongs to the prophecy of the consecrated life, it seems appropriate to give some guidelines so as not to remain imprisoned by fear or laziness. In this sense, we will try to offer some suggestions regarding formative paths, the legal advice needed to move forward, and some advice regarding the ministry of authority so that it may be at the service of a truly communal style of fraternal life. Moreover, we find it necessary to pay special attention to two more topics that are of a sensitive nature in the consecrated life: formation and the communion of goods.

At the basis of every journey, we find it important to underline the need for consecrated men and women to have a new aspiration to holiness, which is unthinkable without a jolt of renewed passion for the Gospel at the service of the Kingdom. We are moved to this journey by the Spirit of the Risen One who continues to speak to the Church through his inspirations.

Pope Francis confirms us in this journey: "For new wine, new wineskins. The newness of the Gospel. What does the Gospel bring us? Joy and newness. To what is new, newness; to new wine, new wineskins. Not to have fear of making changes according to law of the Gospel. This is why the Church asks us, all of us, for a few changes. She asks us to leave aside fleeting structures; they aren't necessary! And get new wineskins, those of the Gospel. The Gospel is newness, the Gospel is a feast. And one can fully live the Gospel only in a joyous heart and in a renewed heart. Room for the laws of the Beatitudes, the joy and freedom that the newness of the Gospel brings us. The Lord gives us the grace of not being prisoners, but the grace of joy and of the freedom which brings us the newness of the Gospel"[18].

---

[18] Francis, *Morning Meditation* in the Chapel of the *Domus Sanctae Marthae*, Rome (5th September 2014).

ONGOING CHALLENGES

11. What Jesus says about resistance to change – because *the old is good* (cf. *Lk* 5:39) – is a phenomenon that we come across in all human operations and cultural systems. As the Gospel teaches in the parables of the good wheat and the darnel (*Mt* 13:25-30) and the dragnet full of *good and bad* fish (*Mt* 13:47-48), good works are often mixed in with those that are not as good. While this is not meant to surprise us, it should keep us continuously vigilant in recognising the limits and fragilities that hinder the processes needed for an authentic and credible witness.

Every stabilised system tends to resist change and work to maintain its position. Sometimes this is done by concealing inconsistencies; at other times, by accepting tarnished old and new, by denying reality and frictions in the name of fictitious harmony, or even by concealing its own objectives through superficial adjustments. Unfortunately, there are plenty of examples of adhesion that is purely formal, while lacking the proper conversion of heart.

VOCATION AND IDENTITY

12. With healthy realism, we must first of all mention the continuously high number of people abandoning the religious life. It is important to shed light on the main reasons for this abandonment, which is taking place both after the early stages of formation (profession, ordination) and at an advanced age. This phenomenon has now been recorded in every cultural and geographic context.

It must be stated clearly that this is not always and only a matter of emotional crises. These emotional crises are often the result of some remote disappointment caused by an inauthentic community life. The difference between what is being put forward in terms of values and what is actually experienced can even lead to a crisis of faith. The excessive number of pressing and exaggeratedly urgent activities may not allow for a solid spiritual life that is capable of nourishing and sustaining the desire for fidelity. In some cases, the isolation of younger members of predominantly elderly communities that struggle to enter into the style of spirituality, prayer and pastoral activity required by the new evangelisation risks weakening their hope for a real promise of life. This frustration can sometimes make abandonment seem like the only way to avoid giving in.

Sociological research has shown that young people do have aspirations towards genuine values that they are willing to commit to seriously. Young people are open to transcendence and are capable of becoming passionate about causes of solidarity, justice and freedom. Through its standardised styles – that are too often out of cultural context – and its perhaps excessive apprehension over managing works, the religious life runs the risk of not intercepting the deepest desire of young people. This creates a gap that renders generational exchange even more difficult and the necessary intergenerational dialogue too hard.

We must, therefore, ask ourselves some serious questions about our formative system. We have certainly made some positive changes in recent years that are taking us in the right direction. These changes, however, have been carried out irregularly and have not modified the structures that are essential in supporting formation. Despite all of the effort and hard work put into formation, it does not seem to reach and truly transform the heart of people. There is the impression that the formation process is more informative than it is performative. The result is that people maintain a certain fragility, both in their existential convictions and in their journey of faith. This leads to minimal psychological and spiritual endurance and the subsequent inability to live one's own mission with openness and courage when it comes to dialogue with culture and social and ecclesial integration.

13. The recent evolution of many institutes has made the problem of integrating different cultures even more acute. Some institutes now find themselves in a situation that is hard to manage: on one side, a few dozen elderly members who are tied to the classic, and sometimes altered, cultural and institutional traditions, and on the other, a large number of young members from different cultures who waver, who feel marginalised, and who no longer accept subordinate roles. The desire to take on responsibilities to get out of a situation of submission could put pressure on some decision-making offices. This can cause experiences of suffering, marginalisation, and misunderstanding that risk putting a strain on the fundamental process of inculturation of the Gospel.

This difficulty in inculturation reveals the growing distance between a classic way of thinking about consecrated life and its standardised forms and the differing way in which it is perceived and desired in emerging ecclesial and cultural contexts. We must take note of the de-westernisation, or de-Europeanisation, of consecrated life that seems to be keeping up with the massive process of globalisation. It is becoming increasingly clear that the most important thing is not the preservation of forms; it is the willingness, in creative continuity, to rethink the consecrated life as the evangelical memory of a permanent state of conversion from which intuitions and concrete choices originate.

FORMATIVE CHOICES

14. Institutes have made considerable effort in this area, also thanks to the help of initiatives from various national and international Conferences of Major Superiors. Despite all this work, there is still little integration between theological and anthropological points of view regarding formation, the formative model and educational pedagogy. This is more than just a theoretical matter because this scarce integration does allow for interaction and dialogue between the two essential and indispensable components of a journey of growth: the spiritual dimension and the human dimension. We can no longer think that these two dimensions act autonomously without being cared for in a complementary and harmonious way.

Caring for the harmonious growth between the spiritual and human dimensions involves paying attention to the specific anthropologies of the various cultures and to the sensibility of new generations, with particular emphasis on life's new contexts. Only a profound new understanding of the symbolism that really touches the heart of new generations can prevent the danger of settling for an adhesion that is only superficial, even trendy, and where it seems that the search for outward signs gives security of identity. The need is becoming urgent for discernment of vocational motivations with emphasis on the different cultural and continental areas[19].

---

[19] Cf. Congregation for Institutes of Consecrated Life and Societies of Apostolic Life, *Starting Afresh from Christ. A Renewed Commitment to Consecrated Life in the Third Millennium* (19th May 2002), 19

15. Even though every institute has been equipped with its own *ratio formationis* in recent years, the application of the formative process is often improvised and belittled. This happens particularly in female institutes where the urgency of their work often takes priority over a fruitful, systematic and organic formative journey. The pressure from their work and commitments to the day-to-day management of the communities runs the risk of creating a detrimental setback in the progress made in the immediate post-conciliar period.

In this perspective, one should avoid inconsistent attendance of theological courses and exclusive attendance of courses for professional degrees, thereby protecting the balance of formation to the consecrated life. In fact, one of the risks is that each person creates his or her own world that is jealously closed off to being shared. This way, in the near future, we will not only have young consecrated people who hold academic titles, but who are also taught, in identification with the values, about the life of *sequela Christi*.

16. Many institutes lack individuals who have the adequate amount of preparation to take on the formative task. This is a rather common issue, especially in smaller institutes that have expanded to other continents. We must always keep in mind that formation cannot be improvised and that it demands remote and continuous preparation. Without a solid formation of the formators, the prepared and trustworthy brothers and sisters of this ministry would not be able to provide the youngest members with real and promising accompaniment. For formation to be effective, it must be based on a strictly personal pedagogy and not limited to just one solution for all values, spiritualities, times, styles and ways. We are faced with the challenge of a personalisation of formation where the initiatory model is recovered. Initiation requires contact between the master and the disciple, walking side by side in trust and hope.

In this context, it is necessary to pay close attention when choosing men and women formators. Their main mission is to convey to those entrusted to them "the beauty of following Christ and the value of the charism by which this is accomplished"[20]. Most importantly, they are required to be "very familiar with the path of seeking God"[21].

---

[20] John Paul II, Post-Synodal Apostolic Exhortation *Vita Consecrata* (25th March 1996), 66.

[21] *Idem.*

All too often, young men and women become prematurely very involved in the management of activities, making it quite difficult to pursue a serious formation. This cannot only be entrusted to those who are directly in charge of the formation of young people, as though it were only their problem; it requires the harmonious and appropriate collaboration and participation of the entire community, the place where "initiation into the hardships and joys of community life takes place"[22]. It is through the fraternal life that one learns to accept others as a gift from God, accepting their positive traits along with their differences and limitations. It is through the fraternal life that one learns to share the gifts received for the building up of all. It is through the fraternal life that one learns the missionary dimension of consecration[23].

There is the risk that continuous formation gets talked about a lot, but that very little is actually done. Organising theoretical courses on theology and covering themes of spirituality is not enough; it is urgent that we develop a culture of permanent formation. This culture should include not only the enunciation of theoretical concepts, but also the ability to review and verify the real lived experience within the community. Furthermore, permanent formation, as an opportunity for reflection and revision, is not to be confused with a sort of religious tourism that is satisfied with simply revisiting the institute's places of origin. There is also the risk of relegating opportunities for formation to special occasions (commemorations for the memories of the institute, celebrations for twenty-five or fifty years of profession), almost as if it were not intrinsic to the dynamism of fidelity in the different stages of life [24].

It is becoming more and more important to include a serious initiation into government in continuous formation. This task, which is so fundamentally important to community life, is sometimes assigned with improvisation and carried out improperly and incompletely.

---

[22] *Ibid*, 67.

[23] Cf. *Idem*.

[24] Cf. *Ibid*, 70-71.

RELATION IN THE *HUMANUM*

Reciprocity between man and woman

17. We are heirs of the ways of life, organisational and governing structures, languages, and collective imagination of a mentality that emphasised profound differences between man and woman, to the detriment of their equal dignity. Even in the Church, and not only in society, numerous unilateral prejudices prevented the recognition of the gifts of the true *genius of women*[25] and the original contribution made by women. This underestimation especially affected consecrated women who were marginalised in the Church's life and pastoral and missionary activity.[26] Post-conciliar renewal saw the emergence and diffusion of an increasing appreciation for the role of women. The twentieth century has been defined as the "Century of Women", mostly because of the awakening of the female conscience in modern culture which was identified fifty years ago by Saint John XXIII as one of the most evident "signs of the times"[27].

Nevertheless, there was an attitude of resistance towards this new sensibility for a long time within the ecclesial community and, at times, even among consecrated women themselves. A particular impetus was recently given by the magisterium itself, encouraging women to embrace this awareness of their dignity. Of particular merit are Popes Paul VI, John Paul II and Benedict XVI who offered valuable magisterium on the subject.

Today, many consecrated women offer positive thoughts that help a biblical vision of *humanun* grow in a society marked by chauvinistic stereotypes in its frame of mind and social, political and religious organisation. Consecrated women offer solidarity to the suffering of women who endure injustice and marginalisation in many world contexts. The contribution made by those who reread the biblical revelation through the eyes of a woman to discover new horizons and styles and to creatively live the "charisms of femininity"[28] is invaluable. The objective of this work of intellect, which is illuminated by faith and

---

[25] Cf. *Ibid*, 58.

[26] Cf. *Ibid*, 57.

[27] John XXIII, Encyclical Letter *Pacem in Terris* on universal peace (11th April 1963), 22.

[28] John Paul II, Apostolic Letter *Mulieris Dignitatem* (15th August 1988), 66.

ecclesial passion, is to promote bonds of fraternity and sorority among consecrated men and women within the Church so as to become a model of anthropological sustainability.

18. Despite the progress we have made on this journey, we must recognise that we have yet to reach a balanced synthesis and a purification of the patterns and models inherited from the past. There are still obstacles in the structures and more than a little misgiving when an opportunity arises to give women "room [...] to participate in different fields and at all levels, including decision-making processes, above all in matters which concern women themselves"[29], in the Church and in the practical management of the consecrated life. Young female vocations carry within them a naturally distinct feminine conscience. Unfortunately, this is not always recognised and embraced as a value. The criticism, through which a certain disapproval is revealed, comes not only from other consecrated women, but also from some men of the Church who maintain chauvinistic and clerical frames of mind. We are far from the message of freedom received from Christ that the Church should "proclaim [...] prophetically, promoting ways of thinking and acting which correspond to the mind of the Lord"[30]. As Saint John Paul II said, and as Pope Francis often reiterates: "Consecrated women therefore rightly aspire to have their identity, ability, mission and responsibility more clearly recognised, both in the awareness of the Church and in everyday life"[31].

True maturation of the reciprocity between man and woman is lacking in the spheres of consecrated life. There is an urgent need for a pedagogy suited to young members for them to find a healthy balance between identity and alterity; just as there is a need for support suited to older members to help them recognise the positive aspects of respectful and peaceful reciprocity. There is cognitive dissonance between old and young religious. For one group, relations between the feminine and the masculine are characterised by reservedness and even phobia, for the other, by openness, spontaneity and naturalness.

---

[29] John Paul II, Post-Synodal Apostolic Exhortation *Vita Consecrata* (25th March 1996), 58.
[30] *Ibid*, 57.
[31] *Idem*.

Another aspect to note is the institutes' weakness *ad intra* concerning this anthropological and cultural process of true integration and mutual complementarity between the feminine and masculine elements and sensibilities. Saint John Paul II considered consecrated women's desire for "room [...] to participate in different fields and at all levels"[32] to be legitimate, yet, in practice, we still have a long way to go. We also run the risk of gravely impoverishing the Church herself, as Pope Francis said: "Let us not reduce the involvement of women in the Church, but instead promote their active role in the ecclesial community. If the Church, in her complete and real dimension, loses women, she risks becoming sterile"[33].

Service of authority

19. The service of authority is not excluded from the current crisis affecting the consecrated life. At first glance, certain situations still show a tendency towards the vertical concentration of the exercising of authority, on both the local and higher levels, thus avoiding the necessary subsidiarity. In some cases, the insistence of some superiors on the personal nature of their authority, almost to the point of thwarting collaboration of the Councils, convinced that they are answering (autonomously) to their own conscience, might seem suspect. Consequently, there is a weak or inefficient co-responsibility in government practices, or even the absence of proper authority. Government may not be centralised in the hands of only one person, thereby circumventing canonical bans[34]. There are still superiors in many institutes who do not take into due account the decisions of their Chapters.

In many cases, the general, provincial and local levels start to blend together because the autonomy that corresponds to the subsidiarity of each level is not guaranteed. Co-responsibility, which leaves room for just autonomy, is not facilitated in this way. We have also noted a phenomenon of superiors who are only worried about maintaining the *status quo*, the idea that "we have always done it this way". Pope Francis's invitation to

---

[32] *Ibid*, 58.

[33] Francis, *Speech* on the occasion of the Meeting with the Bishops of Brazil, Rio de Janeiro (27th July 2013).

[34] Cf. *CIC*, c. 636.

"to be bold and creative in this task of rethinking the goals, structures, style and methods"[35] also applies to government bodies and practices.

20. When it comes to serious matters, it is certainly not a wise practice to resort to majorities that have been established by authority, thereby neglecting convincement and persuasion, correct and honest information, and the clarification of objections. It is even less acceptable to have a government practice that is based on the logic of alliances, especially if it is fuelled by prejudices, as this destroys the charismatic communion of the institutes and negatively affects the sense of belonging. Saint John Paul II did not hesitate to remind us about the ancient wisdom of the monastic tradition – "by the Lord's inspiration, it is often a younger person who knows what is best" (*Regula Benedicti*, III, 3) – for a proper practical exercise in the spirituality of communion which promotes and ensures the active participation of all[36].

No authority figure, not even a founder, must think to be the exclusive interpreter of the charism or to be excluded from the norms of the universal law of the Church. This kind of behaviour can foster and reveal mistrust of the religious family or the community of reference in the other members of the Church[37].

In recent years, and especially in recently founded institutes, there have been episodes and situations of manipulation of the freedom and dignity of people. Not only reducing them to a total dependence that mortified their dignity, and sometimes even their fundamental human rights, but sometimes even leading them, with various means of deception and the pretence of loyalty to God's plans through charism, to a form of submission even in the realms of morality and sexual intimacy: with great scandal for all when the facts are brought to light.

---

[35] Francis, Apostolic Exhortation *Evangelii Gaudium* (24th November 2013), 30.

[36] Cf. John Paul II, Ap. Let. *Novo Millennio Ineunte* (January 6, 2001), 45; Congregation for Institutes of Consecrated Life and Societies of Apostolic Life, Instruction *Starting Afresh from Christ. A Renewed Commitment to Consecrated Life in the Third Millennium* (19th May 2002), 14.

[37] Cf. Congregation for Institutes of Consecrated Life and Societies of Apostolic Life, Instruction *The Service of Authority and Obedience. Faciem tuam, Domine, requiram* (11th May 2008), 13 f.

21. In the day-to-day service of authority, people should not be made to constantly ask permission to carry out normal day-to-day operations. Those who exercise power should not encourage infantile attitudes that can lead to non-responsible behaviours. This path is not likely to lead people to maturity.

Unfortunately, these kinds of situations are more common than many of us are willing to accept and denounce, and are more evident in women's institutes. This is one of the reasons that seems to motivate many people leaving. For some, it is the only response to situations that have become unbearable.

Every request to leave should be an occasion to think seriously about the responsibility of the entire community, superiors in particular. It must be stated clearly that authoritarianism is detrimental to the vitality and fidelity of consecrated people! Canon Law affirms with great courage: "The life of brothers or sisters proper to each institute... is to be defined in such a way that it becomes a mutual support for all in fulfilling the vocation of each"[38].

Therefore, those who exercise their ministry without the patience of listening and the acceptance of understanding give themselves little authoritativeness among their brothers and sisters. Indeed "authority of the religious superior must be characterised by the spirit of service, in imitation of Christ who came not to be served but to serve"[39]. An attitude inspired by Jesus the Servant who washes the feet of his apostles so that they might have a part in his life and in his love[40].

Relational models

22. Commenting on the *new wineskins* that Jesus spoke of in the Gospel, it was said that the substitution of *wineskins* does not happen automatically, but requires effort, skill and willingness to change. In order for this to happen, there must be a generous willingness to renounce every form

---

[38] *CIC*, c. 602; cf. Second Vatican Ecumenical Council, Decree on the Adaptation and Renewal of Religious Life *Perfectae Caritatis*, 15.

[39] Cf. Congregation for Institutes of Consecrated Life and Societies of Apostolic Life, Instruction *The Service of Authority and Obedience. Faciem tuam, Domine, requiram* (11th May 2008), 14b.

[40] Cf. *Ibid*, 12.

of privilege. It is important to remember that nobody, especially those constituted in authority, can be considered exempt from renouncing those models which are, at times, outdated and harmful. No change is possible without renouncing obsolete models[41] so that new horizons and possibilities may arise in government, in common life, in the management of goods, and in mission. We can in no way linger in an attitude that knows more about preserving our ways and attitudes than performing an authentic renewal of them.

A revelatory indication of this impasse is the persistent centralisation of decision-making power and the lack of turnover in the governments of communities and institutes.

We must realise, with evangelical *parresìa*, that, in some female congregations, there is a perpetuation of jobs. Some people remain in government, even in several roles, for too many years. Specific general norms should be put in place to diminish the medium-term and long-term effects of this widespread practice of co-opting into positions of responsibility for members of previous general governments. In other words, regulations that prevent people from holding government positions past their canonical limits, without allowing the use of methods that actually circumvent what the norms are trying to prevent.

23. Another point we cannot hide is that clericalisation of consecrated life has intensified in recent decades; one of the most obvious phenomena is the crisis of numbers in lay religious institutes[42]. There are also many religious presbyters who are dedicated almost exclusively to diocesan life and less so to community life, which is thereby weakened.

Theological and ecclesiological reflection on the figure and function of religious presbyters, especially when they accept a pastoral service remains open.

We should also address the phenomenon of religious and priests who are benevolently welcomed into dioceses by bishops without adequate discernment and the necessary verifications. At the same time, we must

---

[41] Second Vatican Ecumenical Council, Decree on the Adaptation and Renewal of Religious Life *Perfectae Caritatis*, 3.

[42] Cf. Congregation for Institutes of Consecrated Life and Societies of Apostolic Life, *Identity and Mission of the Religious Brother in the Church*, LEV, Vatican City 2013.

keep a check on the ease with which some religious institutes welcome, without adequate discernment, clerical seminarians who have been dismissed by diocesan seminaries or other institutes[43]. These three points can in no way be disregarded, not even to avoid more serious problems for the people and communities involved.

24. Obedience and service of authority are highly sensitive matters, even because the cultures and models have undergone profound and unprecedented transformations that were perhaps disconcerting for some people. In the context in which we live, even the terminology *superiors* and *subjects* is no longer suitable. What worked in a pyramidal and authoritative relational context is no longer desirable or liveable in the sensitivity of communion of our way of feeling like and wanting to be a Church. It must be kept in mind that true obedience always puts obedience to God first, before authority and the person who obeys, just as it refers to the obedience of Jesus; obedience that includes his cry of love *My God, my God, why have you deserted me? (Mt* 27:46) and the Father's loving silence. Pope Francis urges "communities throughout the world to offer a radiant and attractive witness of fraternal communion. Let everyone admire how you care for one another, and how you encourage and accompany one another"[44].

Hence, true obedience does not exclude, but requires that each individual demonstrates his or her own conviction obtained through discernment, even when this conviction does not coincide with what is being asked by a superior. Then, if a brother or sister obeys at his or her own will in the name of communion, even if they see better things, then *charitable obedience*[45] is put into practice.

There is a common impression that the evangelical foundation of fraternity is sometimes missing in the relationship between superiors and subjects. More importance is given to the institution than to the people it is made up of. It is no coincidence, according to the experience of this Congregation, that the main reasons for leaving are: weakening of the

---

[43] Cf. Congregation for the Clergy, *The Gift of Priestly Vocation. Ratio Fundamentalis Institutionis Sacerdotalis* (8th December 2016)

[44] Francis, Apostolic Exhortation *Evangelii Gaudium* (24th November 2013), 99.

[45] Cf. Francis of Assisi, *Admonitions*, III.6.

vision of faith, conflicts in fraternal life, and a life of fraternity that is weak in humanity.

Actually, the way for a superior to guide a community is explained well by Canon Law, as it is in *Perfectae Caritatis*: "Superiors are to exercise their power in a spirit of service [...] govern their subjects as sons or daughters of God and, promoting the voluntary obedience with reverence for the human person, [...] are to strive to build a community of brothers or sisters in Christ, in which God is sought and loved before all things"[46].

25. The relationship between superiors and founders of new foundations merits particular importance and consideration. While we must give thanks to the Holy Spirit for the many charisms that enliven ecclesial life, we cannot hide our perplexity concerning attitudes that often show a narrow conception of obedience, which can become dangerous. In certain cases, infantile subjection and scrupulous dependence are promoted instead of collaboration "with an active and responsible obedience"[47]. This can betray the dignity of a person to the point of humiliation.

The distinction between internal and external forum, in these new experiences or in other contexts, is not always properly considered or respected[48]. Protecting this distinction prevents undue interference which can lead to reduced inner freedom and to psychological subjection, which could then give place to a kind of control of consciences. In these, as in other cases, it is a matter of not inducing excessive dependence in members, which can assume forms of coercion bordering on psychological violence. The roles of the Superior and the founder must also be separated.

26. A levelled community life that does not leave room for originality, responsibility and cordial fraternal relationships, results in little sharing in real life. The extent to which these relations have been compromised can be seen in the practical way of living the evangelical communion of goods, which changes fraternal relationships. Pope Francis warns: "The

---

[46] *CIC*, cc. 618-619; cf. Second Vatican Ecumenical Council, Decree on the Adaptation and Renewal of Religious Life *Perfectae Caritatis*, 14.

[47] Second Vatican Ecumenical Council, Decree on the Adaptation and Renewal of Religious Life *Perfectae Caritatis*, 14.

[48] C. 630 pays special attention to this matter.

current financial crisis can make us overlook the fact that it originated in a profound human crisis: the denial of the primacy of the human person!"[49]

Throughout its long history, consecrated life has always been able to oppose prophetically when economic powers risked humiliating people, especially the poorest people. In this current global financial crisis that Pope Francis often talks about, consecrated people are called to be truly faithful and creative not to fail in prophetic witness to inward common life and to outward solidarity, especially towards the poor and most fragile.

We have passed from a domestic economy to administrative and managerial processes that are getting almost out of control and that highlight our precariousness and, more than that, our unpreparedness. We must immediately focus again on transparency in economic and financial matters as the first step in recovering the authentic evangelical meaning of the real communion of goods within communities and practical sharing of those goods with those who live around us.

27. The distribution of goods in communities must always be done with respect for justice and co-responsibility. In some cases, there is almost a regime that betrays the essential foundations of fraternal life, while "persons in authority are called to promote the dignity of the person"[50]. We cannot accept a management style in which the economic autonomy of a few corresponds to the dependence of others, thereby undermining the sense of reciprocal belonging and the guarantee of fairness, even in the recognition of differences of role and service.

Regulation of the lifestyle of individual consecrated men and women does not excuse them from serious and prudent discernment on the poverty of the institute as evaluation, action and meaningful witness in the Church and among God's people.

28. Consecrated men and women, who are rooted in recognition of the primacy of being over having, and of ethics over economy, should assume an ethic of solidarity and sharing as the soul of their action by preventing

---

[49] Francis, Apostolic Exhortation *Evangelii Gaudium* (24th November 2013), 55.

[50] Congregation for Institutes of Consecrated Life and Societies of Apostolic Life, Instruction *The Service of Authority and Obedience. Faciem tuam, Domine, requiram* (11th May 2008), 13c.

the management of resources from being put exclusively into the hands of a few.

The management of an institute is not a closed circuit; if it were, it would not express ecclesiality. The goods of institutes are ecclesial goods, and serve the same evangelical purpose of promoting the human person, mission, and charitable and supportive sharing with the People of God. A common commitment to concern and care for the poor can give new vitality to an institute.

This solidarity, which is certainly lived within every institute and fraternity, should also be extended to other institutes. In his *Apostolic Letter to all consecrated people*, Pope Francis invites us to "communion between the members of different institutes"[51]. Why not also consider an effective communion in the economic field, particularly with institutes going through times of need, by pooling our resources?[52] It would be a beautiful witness of communion within consecrated life, a prophetic sign in this society of ours in which "a new tyranny is [...] born, invisible and often virtual, which unilaterally and relentlessly imposes its own laws and rules"[53], the tyranny of power and possession which "knows no limits"[54].

---

[51] Francis, *Apostolic Letter* to all consecrated people of the occasion of the Year of Consecrated Life (21st November 2014), II, 3.

[52] Cf. Congregation for Institutes of Consecrated Life and Societies of Apostolic Life, Circular Letter *The guidelines for the management of the Institutes of consecrated life and Societies of apostolic life* (2nd August 2014), 2.3.

[53] Cf. Francis, Apostolic Exhortation *Evangelii Gaudium* (24th November 2013), 56.

[54] *Idem.*

PREPARING NEW WINESKINS

29. Jesus repeatedly warned his disciples against the tendency to leading the newness of the Gospel message back into old habits, while running the risk of reducing it to an *ethos* of pure repetition. With the parable of the *new wine* that must be put into *new wineskins*, we are called to let ourselves be guided by the way of the Beatitudes. The Sermon on the Mount is the *Magna Carta* for the journey of each disciple: *You have learnt how it was said... but I say this to you* (cf. *Mt* 5:21, 27, 33, 38, 43). If this is the direction to move in, the Lord also warns us against every danger of legalistic regurgitation: *Be on your guard...* (*Mk* 8:15; *Mt* 16:11; *Lk* 12:15).

Jesus's words and gestures continuously guide towards a process of infinite openness to the *newness of the Kingdom*. The first step towards this openness is discernment and the refusal of all that is in contradiction with the substantial values of fidelity to God which is manifested in openness to service: *this is not to happen among you* (cf. *Mk* 10:43). The life of Jesus Christ is a story of a *new practice* in which the *new life* of his disciples, who are called to be sensitive to the new logic and new priorities suggested by the Gospel, is rooted.

FAITHFULNESS IN THE SPIRIT

30. The analysis of the ongoing challenges that we presented in the first part of these *Guidelines* must lead us to this evangelical threshold, ready to acknowledge the problematic points so as to open new paths of hope for all. We can apply what Pope Francis recommends: "Pastoral ministry in a missionary key seeks to abandon the complacent attitude that says: 'We have always done it this way'. I invite everyone to be bold and creative in this task of rethinking the goals, structures, style and methods of evangelisation in their respective communities"[55].

It is, therefore, a matter of discovering new *paths* towards authenticity of the evangelical and charismatic witness of the consecrated life. It is a matter of discerning and then starting the necessary processes of purification and healing from the *leaven of malice and wickedness* (cf. *1*

---

[55] Francis, Apostolic Exhortation *Evangelii Gaudium* (24th November 2013), 33

Co 5:8). In this exciting and demanding process, inevitable tensions and suffering can be signs of new development. In fact, we are already at the threshold of new syntheses that will arise with *inward* and *inexpressible groans* (cf. *Rm* 8:23, 26) and with patient exercise of creative fidelity[56].

31. Pope Francis' daily calls for a joyous evangelical spirit without hypocrisies inspire a simplification that finds the faith of the simple and the audacity of saints. The evangelical originality (*Mk* 10:43), of which the consecrated life is meant to be the living prophecy, comes from practical attitudes and choices: the primacy of service (*Mk* 10:43-45) and the steady journey towards the poor and solidarity with the least among us (*Lk* 9:48); the promotion of the dignity of the person in whatever situation they find themselves living and suffering (*Mt* 25:40); subsidiarity as an exercise of reciprocal trust and generous collaboration of all and with all.

32. In order to respond to the calls of the Spirit and the provocations of history, it is good to remember that: "In effect, the consecrated life is *at the very heart* of the Church as a decisive element for her mission, since it 'manifests the inner nature of the Christian calling' and the 'striving of the whole Church as Bride towards union with her one Spouse'"[57]. Hence, consecrated life, in the historic journey of the People of God, is placed in a privileged position in the line of evangelical prophecy. This prophetic line is the sign and result of its charismatic nature that makes it capable of inventiveness and originality. This requires continuous openness to the signs of the Spirit to the point of *listening to the breeze* (cf. *1 K* 19:12). This is the only attitude that allows us to recognise the mysterious paths (cf. *Jn* 3:8) of grace until new hope in the fruitfulness of the Word is reborn (cf. *Jn* 4:35).

33. Identity, with all its magnitude, is not perceived as an immobile and theoretical fact, but as a shared process of growth. The generational gap, inculturation, multiculturalism and interculturalism that increasingly characterise institutes of consecrated life can change from a place of toil to a place of challenging oneself to true community dialogue in cordiality

---

[56] Cf. John Paul II, Post-synodal Apostolic Exhortation *Vita Consecrata* (25th March 1996), 37.
[57] *Ibid*, 3.

and charity of Christ. Only in this way can each person feel involved and responsible in the *community project* "in such a way that it becomes a mutual support for all in fulfilling the vocation of each"[58].

These needs require a change in the structures so they can offer support to all in a renewed trust that revives a dynamic and fraternal faithfulness.

FORMATIVE MODELS AND THE FORMATION OF FORMATORS

34. In recent years, formation has seen a profound transformation of its methods, languages, dynamics, values, goals and stages. Pope Francis reiterated: "We always must think of the People of God in all of this. [...] We must not form administrators, managers, but fathers, brothers, travelling companions"[59], and: "Formation is a work of art, not a police action"[60].

Most institutes adopted their own *ratio formationis* in order to respond to the new requirements. However, there are noticeable differences in language, quality and mystagogical knowledge. The revision of these *rationes*, copied one from the other, has become necessary precisely because formation is so fundamental to the future of consecrated life.

35. In particular, *continuous formation* needs specific care, as the Pope underlined in his famous dialogue with the Superiors General.

a) Continuous formation must be oriented according to the ecclesial identity of consecrated life. It is not just a matter of staying up-to-date on new theologies, ecclesial norms, or new studies relating to the story and charism of one's institute. The task is to strengthen or, often, to find again one's own place in the Church at the service of humanity. This work is often coincides with that classic *second conversion* that is common during life's decisive moments, such as middle age, a moment of *crisis*, or the withdrawal from active life due to illness or old age[61].

---

[58] *CIC*, c. 602.

[59] Francis, *Wake up the World! Conversation with Pope Francis about the Religious Life*, in *La Civiltà Cattolica*, 165 (2014/I), 11.

[60] *Ibid*, 10.

[61] Cf. John Paul II, Post-synodal Apostolic Exhortation *Vita Consecrata* (25th March 1996), 70.

b) We are all convinced that formation must last a lifetime. Nevertheless, we must admit that a culture of continuous formation does not yet exist. This absence is the result of a mentality that is partial and reductive when it comes to continuous formation; hence, sensitivity towards its importance is insufficient and involvement of individuals is minimal. We have yet to find concrete forms, for individuals and communities, that make pedagogical practices a real journey of growth in creative fidelity with significant and lasting outcomes in concrete life.

c) The idea that formation is truly continuous only when it is ordinary and carried out in the reality of everyday life is struggling to catch on. There is still a weak or sociological interpretation of continuous formation that ties it to a simple duty of adaptation or a potential need for spiritual renewal, instead of a continuous attitude of listening and a sharing of calls, problems and horizons. Each individual is called to let himself or herself be touched, educated, provoked, and enlightened by life and by history, by what he or she proclaims and celebrates, by the poor and excluded, and by those near and far.

d) The role of initial formation should also be clarified. It must do more than just educate the young consecrated person on docility and the good customs and traditions of a group; it must render them truly *docibilis*. This means teaching a free heart to learn from the story of each day throughout life in the style of Christ to be of service to all.

e) In reference to this topic, it also becomes indispensable to reflect on the structural and institutional dimension of permanent formation. Just as, after the Council of Trent, seminarians and novices were born for initial formation, today we are called to create forms and structures that support each consecrated person's journey towards the progressive conformation to the sentiments of the Son (cf. *Ph* 2:5). It would be an extremely eloquent institutional sign.

36. Superiors are called to be close to consecrated persons in all issues concerning their journey, both on the personal and community levels. It is the specific task of superiors to accompany, through sincere and

34

constructive dialogue, those in formation or those who find themselves, in various ways, on these paths. The difficulties revealed necessitate the promotion of a fraternal life in which the humanising and evangelical elements find a balance so that each one is co-responsible and, at the same time, considered indispensable for the building of the fraternity. The fraternity is, in fact, the place of eminent continuous formation.

37. New professionalism should also be opportunely prepared in the formation of formators in multicultural contexts. "Good structures help, but of themselves they are not enough"[62]. Interprovincial or international structures aimed at the formation of candidates must take on formators who are really convinced that "Christianity does not have simply one cultural expression, but rather, 'remaining completely true to itself, with unswerving fidelity to the proclamation of the Gospel and the tradition of the Church, it will also reflect the different faces of the cultures and peoples in which it is received and takes root'"[63]. This requires the competence and humility not to impose a cultural system, but rather fertilise every culture with the seed of the Gospel and of our own charismatic tradition while avoiding the "needless hallowing of our own culture"[64].

The synergy of new knowledge and expertise can be good for formative accompaniment within a particular multicultural context. It can help overcome forms of assimilation or homologation that re-emerge in the long run – in the formation process and beyond – and trigger problems that negatively affect the sense of belonging to the institute and perseverance in the vocation to the *sequela Christi*.

TOWARDS EVANGELICAL RELATIONALITY

Reciprocity and multicultural processes

38. Reflecting on feminine consecrated life means asking concrete questions about the institutions and about consecrated women as individuals and as a community, keeping in mind the complexity of our

---

[62] Benedict XVI, Encyclical Letter *Spe Salvi* (30th November 2007), 25.

[63] Francis, Apostolic Exhortation *Evangelii Gaudium* (24th November 2013), 116.

[64] *Ibid*, 117.

time. It should be noted that, in recent years, especially since *Mulieris Dignitatem* (1988), the Magisterium has solicited and accompanied a respectful vision of the cultural and ecclesial processes on feminine identity, which has an obvious (or sometimes latent) affect on life in the institutes.

In particular, cultural diversities force a double path for taking roots in a specific cultural being, as well as the ability to transcend limits of an ever-wider evangelical scope. With religious profession, the consecrated person chooses to mediate between their own specific cultural inscription and their aspirations towards an evangelical life, which inevitably widens their horizons and enhances their sensibility. It is becoming ever more urgent to explore this function of mediation without it being subjected to the particularisms of cultural diversity.

From this perspective, it seems obvious that there is the need to reconsider the theology of the consecrated life in its constitutive elements, accepting the entreaties emerging from the feminine world and joining them together with the masculine world. Emphasis on the specific should not remove belonging to common humanity. It is, therefore, opportune to bring back interdisciplinary approaches, not only in the field of theology, but also in that of human sciences, in their many forms.

39. We must give urgent and focused attention to the recent and hurried process of internationalisation, especially of women's institutes, and the solutions which are often improvised and lacking in prudent gradualness. It must be noted that this geographical expansion has not been accompanied by an adequate revision of the styles, structures, mind-sets and cultural knowledge that are needed for true inculturation and integration. This lack of renewal particularly concerns the importance given to what it is like to be a woman in the Church and in society, as indicated also by the pontifical Magisterium. The insufficient conscientisation, or even worse, the removal of the feminine question has negative consequences with grave damage for younger generations of women. In fact, many women, relying on the institute to introduce them to and educate them in the *sequela Christi*, find themselves obliged to adopt models of behaviour that have become obsolete, especially with regard to roles that know more about "servitude" than they do about service in evangelical freedom.

40. These processes of internationalisation should turn all institutes (men's and women's) into places of sympathetic hospitality where different sensibilities and cultures can gain strength and significance unknown elsewhere and thus, highly prophetic. This sympathetic hospitality is built through honest dialogue among the different cultures so that everybody can convert to the Gospel without renouncing their own distinctive traits. The aim of consecrated life will not be to maintain itself in a permanent state in the different cultures it meets, but to maintain the permanence of evangelical conversion in the heart of the progressive creation of an intercultural human reality.

Sometimes, having a weak and unacculturated anthropological and spiritual view of feminine identity can extinguish or hurt the vitality of the *sodales* present in institutes of consecrated life. There is still a lot of work to do to encourage community models that are suited to the feminine identity of consecrated women. In this regard, the relational structures of discussion and sorority among superiors and sisters must be strengthened. No sister should be relegated to a state of subjection; something that, unfortunately, happens frequently. This state encourages dangerous infantilism, and can hinder a person's overall maturation.

Be vigilant so that the gap between the consecrated women who serve in authority (at all levels) or who are tasked with the administration of goods (at all levels) and the sisters who depend on them doesn't become a source of suffering from disparity and authoritarianism. This happens when the former develop maturity and projectuality, while the latter are deprived of even the most basic forms of decision making and development of personal and community resources.

Service of authority: relational models

41. In the broader view of consecrated life since the Council, we have passed from the centrality of the role of authority to the centrality of the dynamic of fraternity. For this reason, authority must be at the service of communion; a true ministry to accompany brothers and sisters towards conscious and responsible fidelity.

In fact, discussion among brothers or sisters and the listening of individual people becomes an essential place for the evangelical service of authority. The use of managerial techniques, or the spiritualistic and paternalistic application of ways considered to be expressions of "God's will", are reductive with respect to a ministry called to confront the expectations of others, the everyday reality, and the values that are lived and shared in community.

42. The challenge of the relationship between superiors and subjects is the responsible sharing of a common project. This sharing must go beyond the mere execution of those obediences that do not serve the Gospel but only the need to maintain the current situation or respond to administrative, particularly economic, urgencies.

It is in this light that we can consider the request that this Dicastery often receives when it comes time to approve Constitutions (rewrites and/or amendments) to reformulate the current legal terminology regarding the words "superior" and "subject". This is what the conciliar decree *Perfectae Caritatis* explicitly invited us to do when it said: "The manner of living, praying and working should be suitably adapted everywhere to the modern physical and psychological circumstances of the members and also, as required by the nature of each institute, to the necessities of the apostolate, the demands of culture, and social and economic circumstances"[65].

43. We must, therefore, encourage a service of authority that calls us to collaboration and a common view in the style of fraternity. The Dicastery, in tune with the conciliar path, issued the Instruction *The Service of Authority and Obedience. Faciem tuam, Domine, requiram*, recognising that "this theme calls for careful reflection, first of all because of the changes that have taken place in the internal lives of institutes and communities in recent years, and also in light of what more recent Magisterial documents on the renewal of consecrated life have proposed"[66].

---

[65] Second Vatican Ecumenical Council, Decree on the Adaptation and Renewal of Religious Life *Perfectae Caritatis*, 3.

[66] Congregation for Institutes of Consecrated Life and Societies of Apostolic Life, Instruction *The Service of Authority and Obedience. Faciem tuam, Domine, requiram* (11th May 2008), 3.

At this point, more than fifty years after the closing of the Council, the permanence of government styles and practices that are move away from or contradict the spirit of service, to the point of degenerating into forms of authoritarianism, cannot but worry us all.

44. The legitimate prerogative of the personal authority of superiors[67] is, in some cases, mistaken for private authority bordering on misinterpreted protagonism, as Pope Francis admonishes: "Let us think of the damage done to the People of God by men and women of the Church who are careerists, climbers, who 'use' the People, the Church, our brothers and sisters – those they should be serving – as a springboard for their own ends and personal ambitions. These people do the Church great harm"[68]. Moreover, those who exercise the service of authority must guard themselves against "[giving] into the temptation of personal self-sufficiency, [and believing] that everything depends on him or her"[69].

45. Self-referential authority defies the evangelical logic of responsibility among brothers and sisters, weakening the certainties of faith that must guide them[70]. So begins a vicious circle that compromises the vision of faith, an unequivocal prerequisite to the recognition of the role of superiors. This recognition does not merely acknowledge the personality of the person in charge, but goes way beyond that. It is a matter of trusting and entrusting, reciprocally and in truth.

Even in situations of conflict and disagreement, the use of forms of authoritarianism triggers a spiral of misunderstandings and distress that fuels disorientation and distrust within the institute, in other words, doubts regarding the near future of the institute. Those who are called to the service of authority, in whatever situation, cannot fail the sense of responsibility which requires, first and foremost, a balanced sense of one's responsibilities to their brothers and sisters. "All of this is made

---

[67] Cf. *CIC*, c. 618.

[68] Francis, *Address to the Participants in the Plenary Assembly of the International Union of Superiors General* (Rome, 8th May 2013), 2.

[69] Congregation for Institutes of Consecrated Life and Societies of Apostolic Life, Instruction *The Service of Authority and Obedience. Faciem tuam, Domine, requiram* (11th May 2008), 25a.

[70] Cf. Paul VI, Apostolic Exhortation *Evangelica Testificatio* (29th June 1971), 25.

possible by confidence in the responsibility of the brothers or the sisters 'promoting the voluntary obedience of their subjects with reverence for the human person', and through dialogue keeping in mind that bonding must come about 'in a spirit of faith and love in the following of the obedient Christ' and not for other motivations'[71].

46. "Superiors, constituted for a definite time, do not remain too long in offices of governance without interruption"[72]. This norm of Canon Law is still in the reception process; there are considerable variables in institutional practices. The justifications commonly adopted to extend one's mandate beyond the limits established by proper right concern emergencies or a lack of resources, with specific reference to local communities. The influence of institutes' traditions has helped stabilise certain mentalities that hinder alternation. This ends up transforming a role of service into the keeping of a position. In this perspective, if the norms dictated by proper right are unsuitable, they must be revised; if they are clear in their direction, they must be respected.

Careful evaluation of the slowdown in the turnover of superiors seems to be more present in the preoccupation to ensure the administrative continuity of work, and less so when the community's need for religious and apostolic animation is concerned. Moreover, the presence of younger generations of brothers and sisters in a community sets the conditions for generational change. Delay in alternation could be interpreted as distrust in their skills and abilities to the point of creating a gap that might later prove to be unbridgeable.

47. We must all remember what Pope Francis said on this topic: "In the consecrated life we live the encounter between the young and the old, between observation and prophecy. Let's not see these as two opposing realities! It's good for the elderly to communicate their wisdom to the young; and it's good for the young people to gather this wealth of experience and wisdom, and to carry it forward, not so as to safeguard it

---

[71] Congregation for Institutes of Consecrated Life and Societies of Apostolic Life, Instruction *The Service of Authority and Obedience. Faciem tuam, Domine, requiram* (11th May 2008), 14b.

[72] *CIC*, c. 624 § 2.

in a museum, but to carry it forward addressing the challenges that life brings, to carry it forward for the sake of the respective religious orders and of the whole Church"[73].

Service of authority: Chapters and Councils

48. In this continuous work of discernment and renewal, particular importance is given to "Chapters (or similar meetings), whether particular or general, at which institutes are called to elect superiors according to the norms set out in their Constitutions, and to discern, in the light of the Spirit, the best ways to preserve and adapt their charism and their spiritual patrimony to changing historical and cultural situations"[74]. Furthermore, the Chapter "is to be composed in such a way that, representing the entire institute, it becomes a true sign of its unity in charity"[75].

Reflection on Chapter representation starts from its most authentic horizon: unity in charity. The rules and procedures for electing sisters and brothers to Chapters – particularly at the general level – cannot disregard the new cultural and generational makeup of many institutes of consecrated life and societies of apostolic life today. This multicultural dimension must be expressed in a fair and balanced way in the Chapter's composition.

49. The problem is revealed when rules and procedures are unsuitable or obsolete, resulting in an imbalance of representation and the risk of exposing the Chapter's composition to improper cultural hegemonies or restricted generational representation. As to avoid these distortions, we must gradually include the representation of sisters and brothers from different cultural areas. We must also put trust in those who, in our world, are considered too young, but who, in other civil and cultural environments, would have qualifications to take on remarkable responsibilities. Procedures should be made more flexible in order to guarantee broader and more forward-thinking representation to guarantee a hopeful and liveable future.

---

[73] Francis, *Homily* on the Feast of the Presentation of the Lord on the occasion of the 18th Day of Consecrated Life, Rome (2nd February 2014).

[74] John Paul II, Post-synodal Apostolic Exhortation *Vita Consecrata* (25th March 1996), 42.

[75] *CIC*, c. 631 § 1

We are not only talking about the correctness of procedures and the intelligent docility to the choices of method; it is a matter of "seeking all light possible on the will of Christ for the ongoing life of the community", as *The Rule of Taizé* writes, in a spirit of searching that is purified by the sole desire to discern God's plan.

50. Every decision that is made in the heart of the assembly must be accompanied by the will of each capitular, which is open to the Spirit. This will does not disdain the exchange of contributions and points of view because, while they are different, they contribute to the search for the truth. In this way, the tension towards unanimity and the possibility of reaching it are not utopian goals, but instead express the clearest product of listening and common openness to the Spirit.

It would not be prudent to relegate discernment to the private horizons of capitulars, as if the Chapter were the undertaking of solitary individuals. It is a matter of "[making] contact with the Spirit", and this means "[listening] to what God is telling us within our situations" in the institutes. Discernment "does not stop at describing the various situations, the problems [...] but which always goes a step further and is able to see an opportunity, a possibility behind every face, every story, every situation"[76]. We must not forget that the General Chapter is a place of personal and unanimous obedience to the Holy Spirit; this docile listening is invoked by bowing our intelligence, heart and knees in prayer. In this conversion, at the time of the decision, each capitular acts in conscience and judges, by the light of the Holy Spirit, the good of the institute within the Church. This attitude of prayerful obedience is a constant in the history of General Chapters, which for good reason started on the day of Pentecost.

51. This Chapter event also involves the election of the Superior General. In recent years, there has been a certain tendency to resort to postulation. An institute is regulated by canons 180-183 of the *Code of Canon Law*. Postulation is used in cases where there is some impediment to the canonical election of the same person or in cases of the dispensation of personal requisites inherent to the role as determined by universal or proper law, such

---

[76] Francis, *Address* on the occasion of the Pastoral Congress of the Diocese of Rome (16th June 2016).

as age and years of profession[77], or relative incompatibility of offices[78]. The most common case is the impediment of a new election (or confirmation) of the Superior General after the term of office outlined by the Constitutions has ended. These particular cases present connotations of the complexity of contexts (institutes), personal situations (candidates already in office), and last but not least, contingencies that direct towards requesting postulation from the competent Dicastery. Some directions are specified.

Taking postulation for granted, as if other possible alternatives were excluded *a priori*, is not the best premise for elective discernment. The required majority is "at least two-thirds of the votes"[79]. This canonical disposition is meant to encourage discernment before resorting to postulation. Co-responsibility exercised collectively also entails the responsibility to explore alternative solutions. Some institutes have introduced a process of informal preliminary consultations into their practice. The suggested guideline should prevent the formation of pre-established majorities; otherwise it's a short step from taking postulation for granted.

52. In addition to the Supreme Moderator[80], General Chapters also ordinarily elect the council, which is the collaborative body in the institute's government. "A personal and confident participation in the community's life and mission is required"[81] of each councillor: "Participation which allows for the exercise of dialogue and discernment"[82], in the spirit of sincerity[83] and loyalty "in order to ensure the constant presence of the Lord who enlightens and guides"[84].

---

[77] Cf. *CIC*, c. 623.

[78] Cf. *CIC*, c. 152.

[79] Cf. *CIC*, c. 181 § 1.

[80] Cf. *CIC*, c. 625 § 1.

[81] Congregation for Institutes of Consecrated Life and Societies of Apostolic Life, Instruction *Starting Afresh from Christ. A Renewed Commitment to Consecrated Life in the Third Millennium* (19th May 2002), 14.

[82] *Idem*.

[83] Cf. *CIC*, c. 127 § 3.

[84] Congregation for Institutes of Consecrated Life and Societies of Apostolic Life, Instruction *Starting Afresh from Christ. A Renewed Commitment to Consecrated Life in the Third Millennium* (19th May 2002), 14.

If the inevitable difficulties and misunderstandings are not addressed in time, they can compromise the will to understand and the capacity for convergence within the council. When caring for the common good of the institute, a collaborative body in the government commits to taking care of its operation. This also means not neglecting those means of accompaniment (spiritual, professional, and of specific formation) that set the premise for forward-thinking discernment. Indeed, the council must not make taking care of its image the first priority; it should worry about its credibility as a collaborative body in the government of the institute, above all else.

53. The new geography of the presence of consecrated life in the Church is drawing new cultural balances in the lives and governments of institutes[85]. The international composition of a chapter usually expresses the multicultural configuration of the council as well. Many institutes of consecrated life and societies of apostolic life already have a long tradition in this regard. Newer institutes are in a period of apprenticeship to learn how to "make present in Catholic unity the needs of different peoples and cultures"[86]. It is a demanding journey that "needs purification and growth"[87].

The recent processes of internationalisation offer the chance for a future that does not improvise in matters concerning formation for roles of responsibility, and especially, the assumption of the role of councillor. The generational and cultural change should not allow for situations that can compromise the inner dynamics of conciliar discernment and in consequence, the good governance of the institute.

Some examples of problematic situations are: individuals who are suitable, but not yet sufficiently prepared, or who have been made candidates prematurely; religious who are co-opted more for cultural distribution than for their personal experience and/or expertise; last but not least, choices that are made from a lack of alternatives.

---

[85] Cf. *Ibid*, 17.

[86] John Paul II, Post-synodal Apostolic Exhortation *Vita Consecrata* (25th March 1996), 47.

[87] Francis, Apostolic Exhortation *Evangelii Gaudium* (24th November 2013), 69.

54. The introduction of brothers and sisters from other cultures and generations certainly does not change the traditional role of the council, however, it affects how the role is perceived and how it interacts inside and outside of the council. The different points of view (analysis/assessment of problems) broaden the horizon of understanding of the realities of the institute: more from the peripheries than from the centre. Cultures and generational change – an already complex combination – should foster new enthusiasm to face a sustainable future within the institute.

The initiation into a role of responsibility is a part of experience. If experience is a daily learning process, that learning process must be supported by specific formation. Otherwise, one's experience will not permit the full effectiveness of the role itself and its integration into the dynamics of the council. We must in this case rediscover, or rethink, the guidelines that have been developed throughout the history of the government of institutes of consecrated life and societies of apostolic life, which prepared for the future by investing in the present and standing the test of time. The near future cannot narrow the horizon: new professionalism (knowledge and skills) can make contributions that broaden our horizons and, more importantly, keep us from being marginalised by the future, like short-sighted prisoners who, in the long run, immobilise the overall journey.

CONCLUSION

55. In these decades of conciliar renewal, consecrated men and women have worked with generous commitment and boldness in the vineyard of the Lord. It is now time for the harvest, and for *new wine* to be joyfully squeezed from the grapes and diligently collected in the right *wineskins* until the fermentation that comes with ageing sediments, leaving room for new stability. *New wine* and *new wineskins* are at our disposal and were created by our collaboration according to the charisms and the ecclesial and social circumstances, under the guidance of the Spirit and Church leaders. The time has come to preserve the newness in creativity, so that the genuine flavour of the fruitfulness that is blessed by God can be conserved.

New wine requires the ability to go beyond the models we have inherited in order to appreciate the newness brought on by the Spirit, to accept it with gratitude, and to guard it, not just temporarily, but until the fermentation has finished. Even the *new cloak* that Jesus speaks about on the same page of the Gospel has been sewn up through the various phases of adaptation, and the time has come to wear it with joy among the believers.

56. The *new wine*, *new wineskins* and *new cloak* indicate a season of maturity and completeness that cannot be jeopardised by hasty combinations or strategic compromises: *old* and *new* should not be mixed because each one belongs to its own season, is the product of different times and arts, and should be preserved in its own genuineness.

The Master of the vineyard, who has made fruitful the work of our hands and guided our journey of adaptation, shows us how to preserve the newness that has been entrusted to us through suitable means and patient vigilance, without fear and with renewed evangelical enthusiasm.

57. Holy Mary, *Woman of the new wine*, guard the desire in us to go forward in obedience to the newness of the Spirit, recognising the sign of his presence in the *new wine*, fruit of harvests and new seasons.

Make us docile to your grace and diligent in preparing *wineskins* that may contain and not waste the fermentation of the juice of the vine. Make firm our steps in the mystery of the cross that the Spirit requires for every new creation.

Teach us to do as Christ your Son will tell us (cf. *Jn* 2:5), so as to sit at his table each day: he is the new wine through which we give thanks and receive and give blessing.

Nourish in us hope, in expectation of the day when we will drink the new fruit of the vine with Christ in the Kingdom of the Father (cf. *Mt* 26:29).

The Holy Father approved the publication of these Guidelines during an Audience on 3rd January 2017.

Vatican City, 6th January 2017, *Epiphany of the Lord*

Cardinal João Braz de Aviz
Prefect

✠ **José Rodríguez Carballo, O.F.M.**
Archbishop Secretary